The Baby Swans

Written by Marilyn Woolley

Illustrated by Susy Boyer

Flying Start
to Literacy®

Contents

Chapter 1: The swans' new home

One day at the end of winter, two large, white swans came to the clean, clear waters of the wetland.

The swans were looking for a good place to lay their eggs. They needed a place with lots of food to eat. They needed a place where they could protect their babies from foxes.

As the swans swam around the wetland, they saw that many reeds grew in the water. The swans needed the reeds to make a nest. There were many water plants for the swans to eat.

In the rushes, the fox was waiting. The fox could only get the swans if they came onto the land.

Chapter 2: Danger lurks

The swans worked hard to make a safe nest for their eggs in the middle of the wetland.

The father swan pulled up long reeds and plants from the water. The mother swan used her beak and her long, thin neck to lay these reeds on top of each other.

It took the swans two weeks to finish their large nest on top of the water.

When the nest was finished, the mother swan laid five large green eggs in the nest.

She covered these eggs with her warm feathers. She tucked her long neck under her wing and rested.

The fox sat and watched the swans.

He could not attack a fully grown swan, but swan eggs and baby swans were his favourite food. The fox licked his lips and slipped away.

Chapter 3: Keeping safe

While the mother swan kept the eggs warm, the father swan fed on water plants. Sometimes he would dive to the bottom of the water to get the roots of the plants to eat.

When he came back to the nest, he put more reeds on the nest and took his turn sitting on the eggs. The mother swan left the nest to feed on water plants.

Hiding in the reeds, the fox watched the swans.

After about six weeks, there were cracks in the eggs and pieces of shell slowly began to fall off them. At last, five little swans hatched from the eggs.

The mother and father swan took turns bringing food to the babies, but they never left them alone. They knew that the babies could not protect themselves.

Chapter 4: Attack!

The next day, the baby swans left the nest. The fox was hidden in the reeds, watching and waiting.

The baby swans could already swim. They followed their parents around the wetland. But the littlest baby could not keep up.

He cheeped and cheeped but his mother and father did not hear him.

Just as the fox was about to spring out and snatch the baby swan with his sharp teeth, the mother swan turned and saw the fox in the reeds. She flapped her wings and clacked her beak. She swam straight at the fox, hissing and hissing.

The mother swan was too big for the fox to fight. He turned and ran. The baby swan was safe.

Chapter 5:
Leaving the wetlands

During summer, the baby swans grew new white feathers and their beaks turned dark orange.

When winter came, the swans stood tall and flapped their wings just like their mother and father did.

With a spray of water, the swans flew away from the wetland.

The mother and father swans left the wetland, too. As they flew away, they made a deep trumpet-like call.

The swans would return to the same clean wetland to begin a new family next year.

Hidden in the reeds, the fox watched
them go.

A note from the author

Every day when I walked my dog along the path near our wetland, I would watch as the swans made a nest from the reeds in the middle of the wetland. When the baby swans hatched out, I used to enjoy watching them grow as they ate plants in the water.

As they grew bigger, they would flap their wings to make them stronger and stay safe from the foxes. I was sad when they learnt to fly by themselves, but I knew next year there would hopefully be another group of new baby swans.